THE
ART DECO STYLE

IN
HOUSEHOLD OBJECTS
ARCHITECTURE
SCULPTURE
GRAPHICS
JEWELRY

468 AUTHENTIC EXAMPLES
SELECTED BY
THEODORE MENTEN

DOVER PUBLICATIONS, INC.
NEW YORK

Published in Canada by General Publishing Company, Ltd., 30 Lesmill Road, Don Mills, Toronto, Ontario.
Published in the United Kingdom by Constable and Company, Ltd.

"The Art Deco Style" is a new work, first published by Dover Publications, Inc. in 1972. The plates are reproduced from the following books: the series (in many portfolios) "L'Art International d'Aujourd'hui," Editions d'Art Charles Moreau, Paris, c. 1929–1931; H. Clouzot, "La Ferronnerie Moderne," Editions d'Art Charles Moreau, Paris, 3 portfolios, n.d.: Henri Martinie, "Exposition des Arts Décoratifs, Paris, 1925: La Ferronnerie," Editions Albert Lévy, Paris, 2 portfolios, 1926 and 1929; H. Rapin, "La Sculpture Décorative Moderne," Editions d'Art Charles Moreau, Paris, n.d.; H. Rapin, "La Sculpture Décorative à l'Exposition des Arts Décoratifs de 1925," Editions d'Art Charles Moreau, Paris, n.d.

The publisher gratefully acknowledges the cooperation of the Buffalo and Erie County Public Library which supplied much of the material reproduced in this volume.

International Standard Book Number: 0-486-22824-X
Library of Congress Catalog Card Number: 72-78867

Manufactured in the United States of America
Dover Publications, Inc.
180 Varick Street
New York, N. Y. 10014

INTRODUCTION

Although Art Deco derives its name from the great 1925 Paris exhibition, "L'Exposition Internationale des Arts Décoratifs et Industriels Modernes," the term is now generally applied to the typical artistic productions of the 1920's and 1930's. It might best be characterized as an attempt to unite arts with industry, embracing the machine age and repudiating the old antithesis of "fine" and "industrial" art.

The 1925 exhibition, which was planned to exclude all copies and imitations of ancient styles, did not meet with immediate approval among progressive observers. Le Corbusier and his colleagues, in fact, built their own pavilion of protest at the edge of the exhibition. Yet within two years the prismatic geometric style consecrated by the exhibition had found its way into every area of modern life. Large public buildings, furniture, lighting fixtures, book bindings and jewelry all bore the same unifying elements that labeled them as Art Deco.

The sources of Art Deco, which included Egyptian and Mayan art, Cubism, Fauvism and Expressionism, are clearly seen in this selection of plates. Henri Sauvage's design for an apartment complex to be built on the banks of the Seine (plate 70) is reminiscent of a Mayan temple in the Yucatan. Raymond Templier's design for a necklace (plate 161) might almost have come from King Tut's tomb. It is clear that the Martels could not have designed the multi-faceted mirror for the foyer of their Parisian home (frontispiece) without the inspiration of the Cubism of a Picasso or a Braque.

The chief force underlying all Art Deco is its emphasis upon geometric patterns. Whether we observe the garden of the house designed by Moreaux (plate 4) Dudok's schools (plate 73) or Vuitton's cut-crystal and ebony bottles (plate 144), the geometric shapes are obvious. The sculptures by Csaky (plates 105, 107) are considered in the same category as the elevator shaft in the Grunfeld Department Store (plate 44) or the lighting fixtures at the Gipsen Factory (plate 52).

These plates, taken from a number of books published shortly after the 1925 exhibition, are authentic documents of the best work done during this period. The main source is the 20-volume collection "L'Art International d'Aujourd'hui" (International Art of Today) published in Paris by Charles Moreau. Each volume in this collection was edited by a practicing artist of the time. Robert Mallet-Stevens, whose architectural works (such as those in plates 16-19, 25, 28, 38, 94, 121, 178) are the essence of Art Deco, chose the photographs for the volume on large buildings. André Lurçat, who designed the townhouse in plate 12 and the furniture in plate 37, edited the volume of terraces and gardens. Pierre Chareau, whose interior design of the Mallet-Stevens townhouse at Hyères appears in plate 17, edited the volume on furniture.

My choice of plates has been governed by the desire to give not only the best possible examples of Art Deco, but also representative works by some of the outstanding exponents of the style. No book on Art Deco would be complete without the silver of Jean Puiforcat (plates 101, 142), the sculpture of Joël and Jan Martel (plates 177-179), a screen by Edgar Brandt (plate 57), a tea service of Gérard Sandoz (plate 147) or the jewelry of Jean Fouquet (plates 155 and 158–160).

Art Deco is today enjoying a revival. Not only have such prestigious galleries as The Minneapolis Institute of Arts and the Finch College Museum mounted Art Deco exhibits, but graphic designers, package designers, and advertisers have found the motifs of Art Deco a valuable source of creativity. I have selected the plates in this book of designs of the 20's and 30's to appeal to the nostalgic reader and to serve as an inspiration to the designer of the 70's.

THEODORE MENTEN

CONTENTS

1. (Top) Garden, Lyons. Tony Garnier, architect. (Bottom) Garden, Hyères. Gabriel Guévrékian, architect.

2. Terrace of a private home, Garches. Le Corbusier and P. Jeanneret, architects.

3.   Terrace of a villa, Neuilly, Gabriel Guévrékian, architect.

4. Garden and terraces, Saint-Cloud. J. Charles Moreux, architect.

5. Garden of the Coonley Playhouse, Riverside, Illinois. Frank Lloyd Wright, architect.

6. Bauhaus faculty residences, Dessau. Walter Gropius, architect.

7. Private residence, Hyères. Robert Mallet-Stevens, architect.

8.   Private villa, Neuilly. Guévrékian and Denis, architects.

9.   Two townhouses. Raymond Nicolas, architect.

10. Two views of a private residence, Breslau. Adolf Rading, architect.

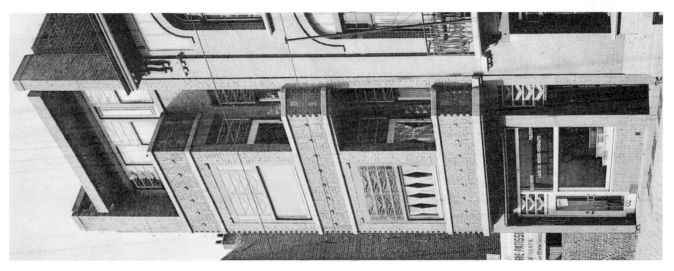

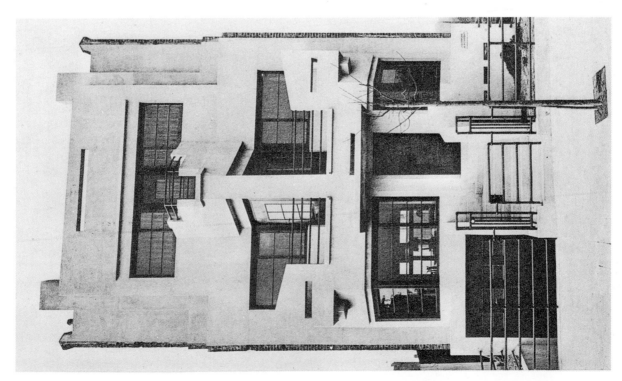

11. (Left) Private residence. J. Diongre, architect. (Middle) Private residence, Uccle. P. Rubbers, architect. (Right) Store. H. A. Van Anrooy, architect.

12. (Top) Townhouse, Paris. André Lurçat, architect. (Bottom) Townhouse, Versailles.
André Lurçat, architect.

13. Two views of a villa, Hamburg. Block and Hochfild, architects.

14. Two views of a villa, Loverval. H. and M. Leborgne, architects.

15. Two views of a villa, Cologne. Walter Reitz, architect.

16. Two views of a townhouse, Hyères. (Top) Terrace. (Bottom) Reception room. Robert Mallet-Stevens, architect.

17. Two views of a townhouse, Hyères. (Left) Detail of the reception room showing a writing desk. (Right) View of the reception room. Interior design by Pierre Chareau. Robert Mallet-Stevens, architect.

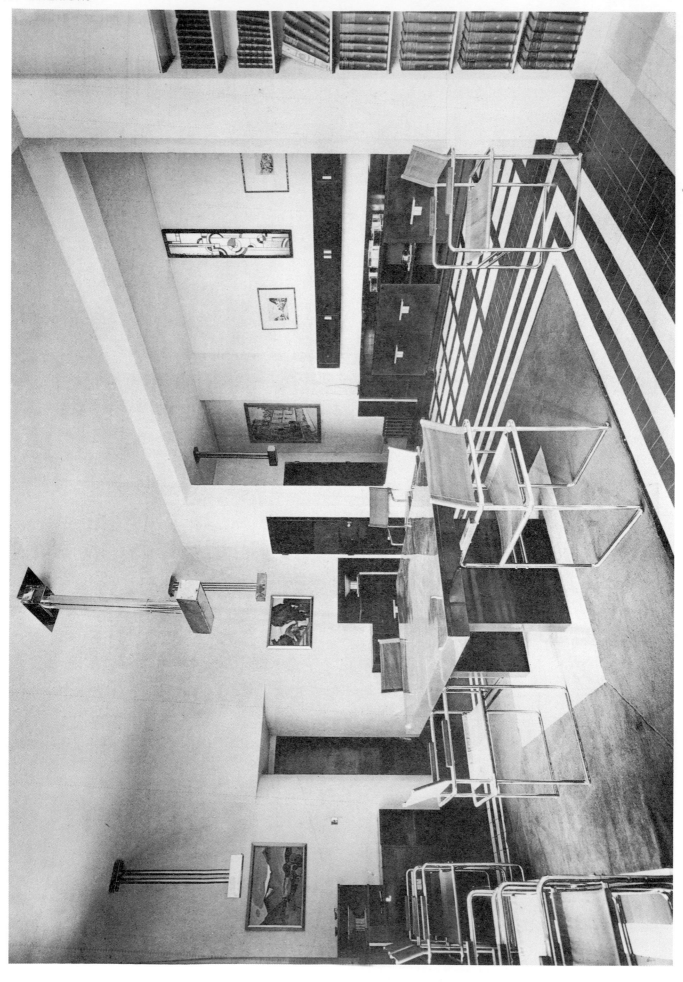

18. Dining room. Robert Mallet-Stevens, architect.

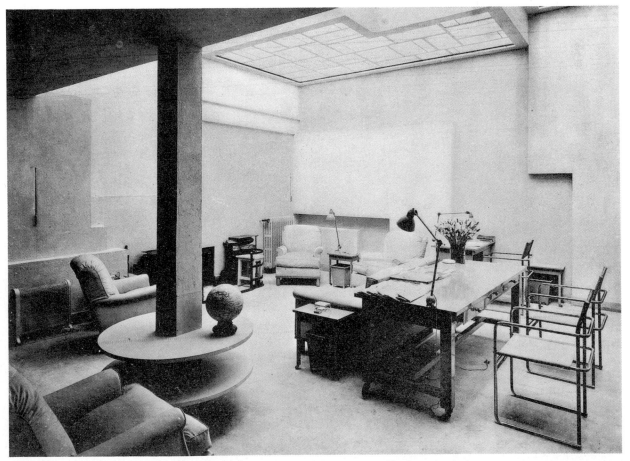

19. Two views of a studio. Robert Mallet-Stevens, architect.

20.   Bedroom and dining room. Djo-Bourgeois, architect.

21.   Study in a private residence, Paris. Gabriel Guévrékian, architect.

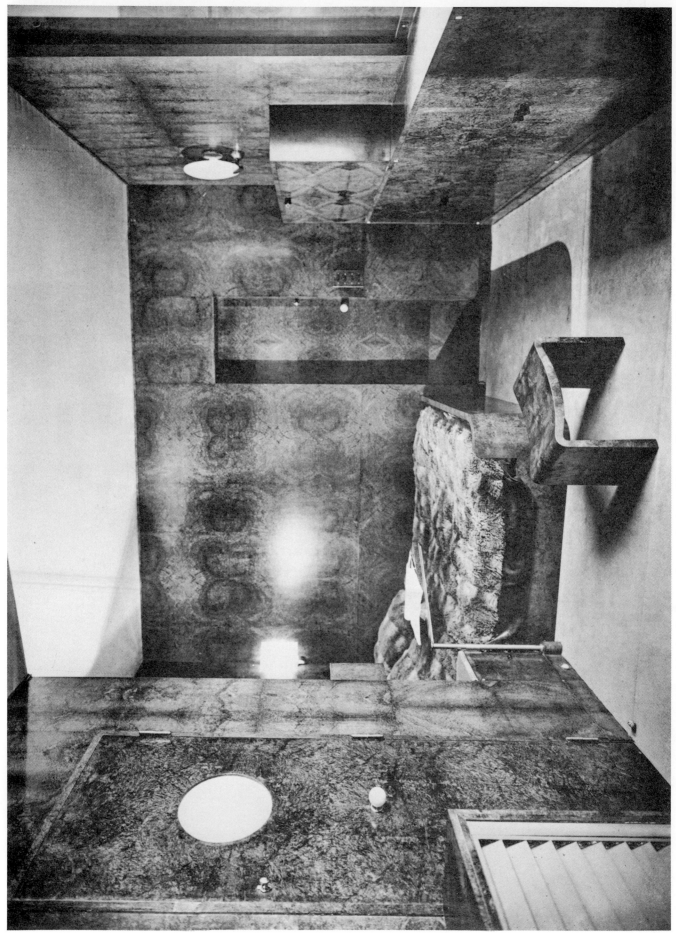

22.   Master bedroom in a private residence, Paris.   Gabriel Guévrékian, architect.

23. (Top) Small apartment. Bohus Kupka, architect. (Bottom) Living room. Oldricht Stary, architect.

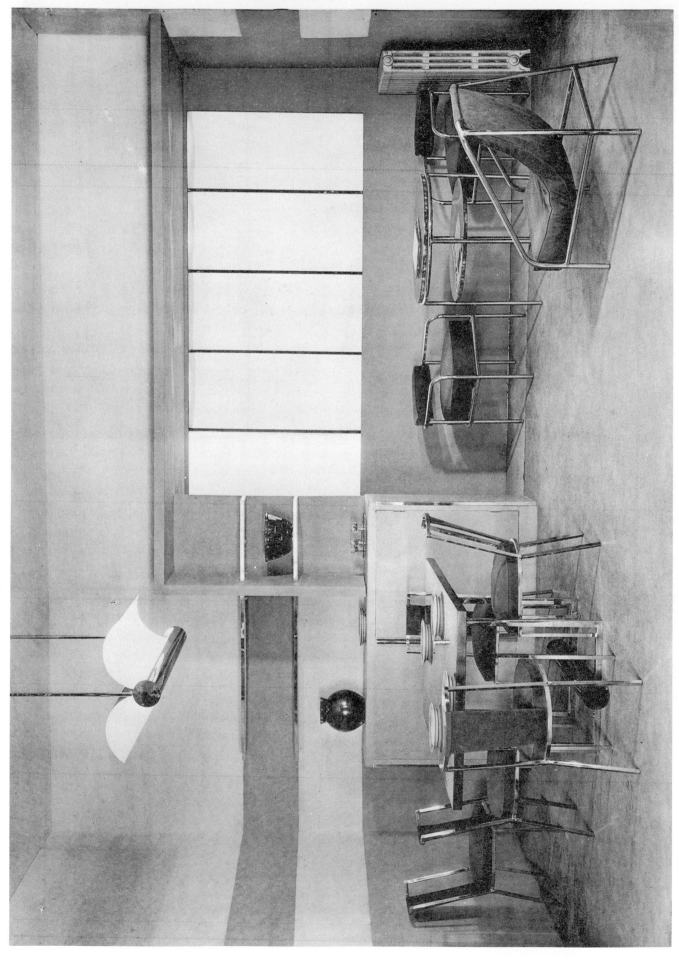

24. Dining room. René-Herbst, designer.

25.   Detail of the studio in the Martel House, Paris. Robert Mallet-Stevens, architect.

26. Detail of a bathroom in a Paris townhouse. Gabriel Guévrékian, architect.

27. Interior details. Raymond Nicolas, architect.

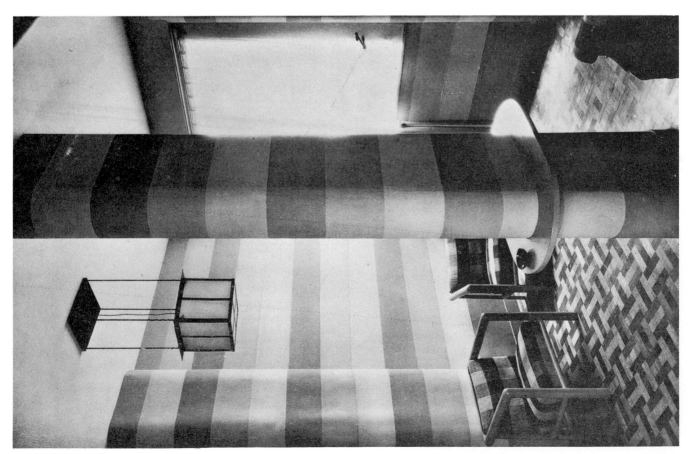

28. Interior details. Robert Mallet-Stevens, architect.

29. (Left) Interior detail of a bar. Louis Sognot, designer. (Right) Interior detail. M. Guillemard, designer.

30. Crypt. Henry Rosenthal, architect.

31. (Left) Detail of a dressing table. Henry Rosenthal, architect. (Right) Vestibule. Henry Rosenthal, architect.

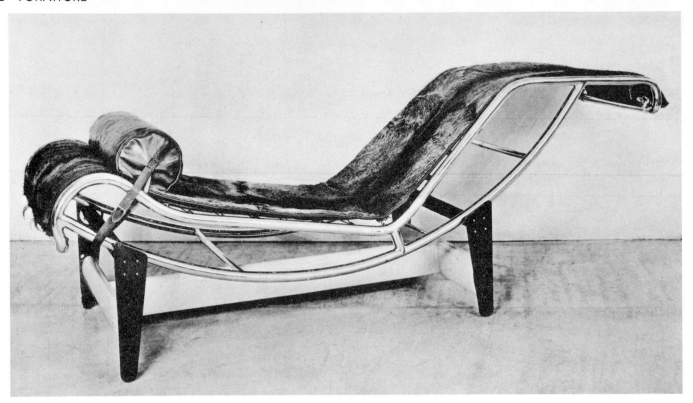

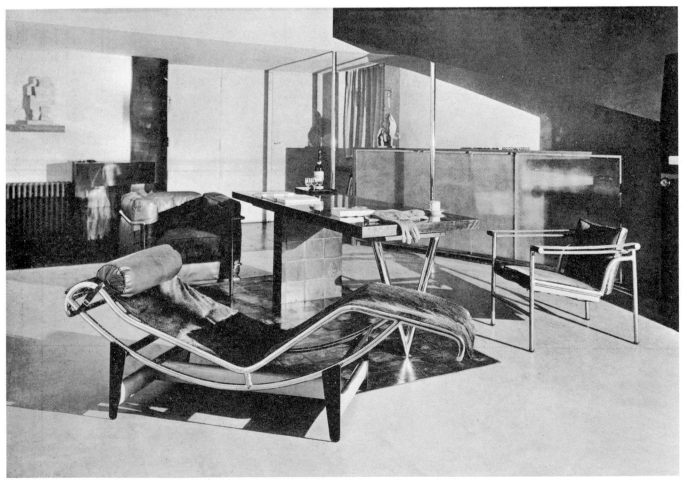

32.   Le Corbusier, P. Jeanneret, Charlotte Perriand.

33.   Le Corbusier, P. Jeanneret, Charlotte Perriand.

34. Eileen Gray.

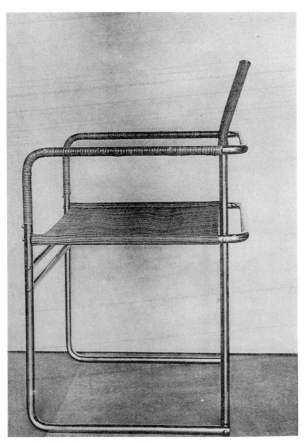

35.   Marcel Breuer.

36.   Marcel Breuer.

37. André Lurçat.

38. (Top) S. Lipska and Martin. (Bottom left) Pierre Legrain. (Bottom right) Robert Mallet-Stevens.

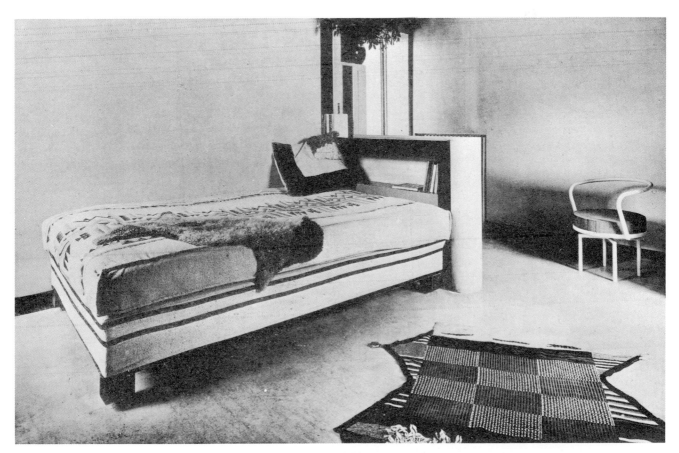

39.   Charlotte Perriand.

40.   (Top) Jaromir Krejcar.   (Bottom) Hanazaveska.

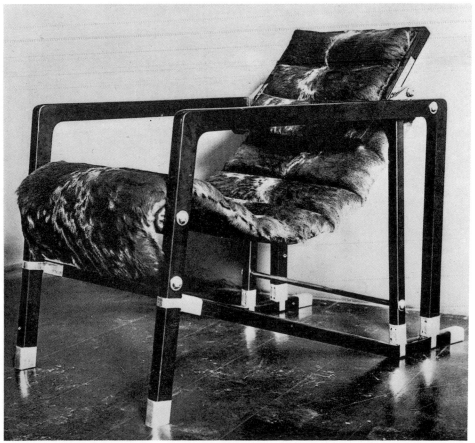

41. Eileen Gray.

42.   René-Herbst.

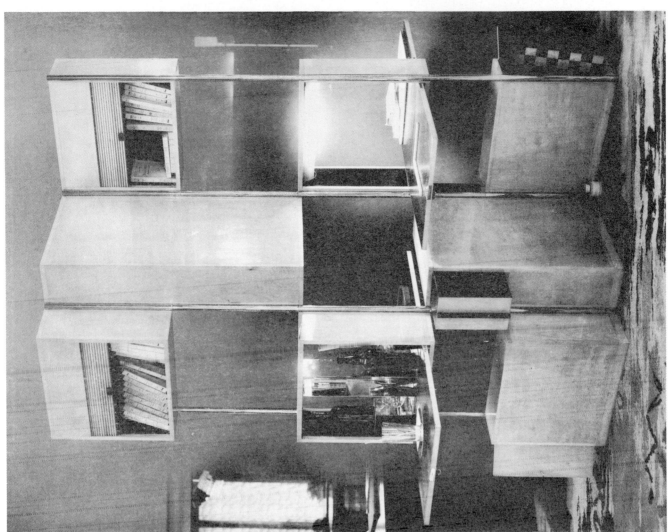

43. Louis Sognot.

44.   Elevator shaft in the Grunfeld Department Store, Berlin. Otto Firle, architect.

45.   Lighting fixtures designed by J. Le Chevalier. R. Koechlin, assistant.

46.   Lighting fixtures designed by J. Le Chevalier. R. Koechlin, assistant.

47. (Top) Letters. René-Herbst, architect. (Middle) Letters. Ch. Siclis, architect. (Bottom) Letters. F. Lévèque, architect. R. Cognéville, designer.

48. Enzel's Shoe Store. Raymond Nicolas, architect. Pargade, designer of ironwork.
(Top) Storefront. (Bottom) Detail of the front grillwork viewed from the inside.

49.   Skylight at the Palace of Beer, Nancy. Jean Prouvé, designer of ironwork.

50. (Top) Balustrade at the Paramount Theatre, Paris. A. Bluysen and J. P. Mangeaut, architects. Raymond Subes, designer of ironwork. (Bottom) Interior grillwork. Raymond Subes, designer of ironwork. Maurice Jallot, designer.

51. Auto-Pleyela (player-piano) designed by Pierre Legrain and built at the Pleyel Piano Company, Paris.

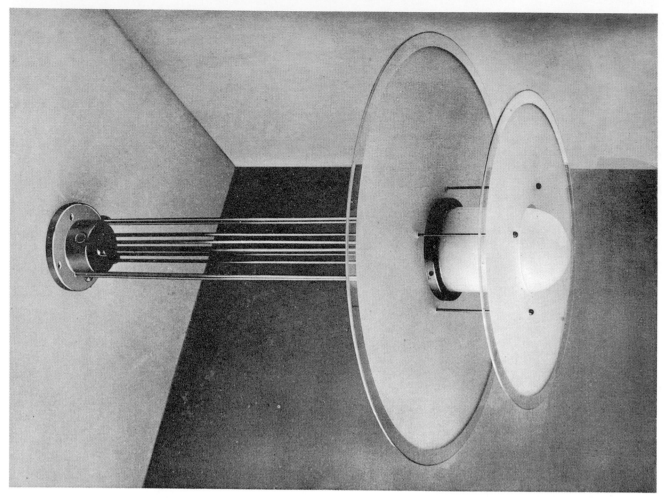

52. Lighting fixtures at the Gipsen Factory, Rotterdam.

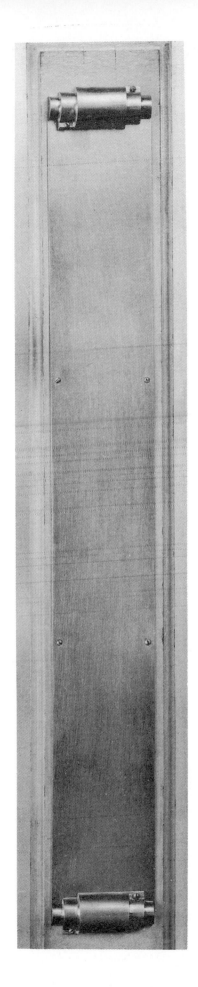

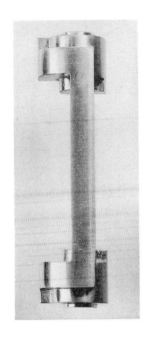

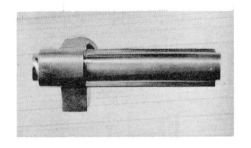

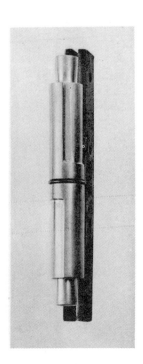

53.   Locks, designed by R. Cognéville.

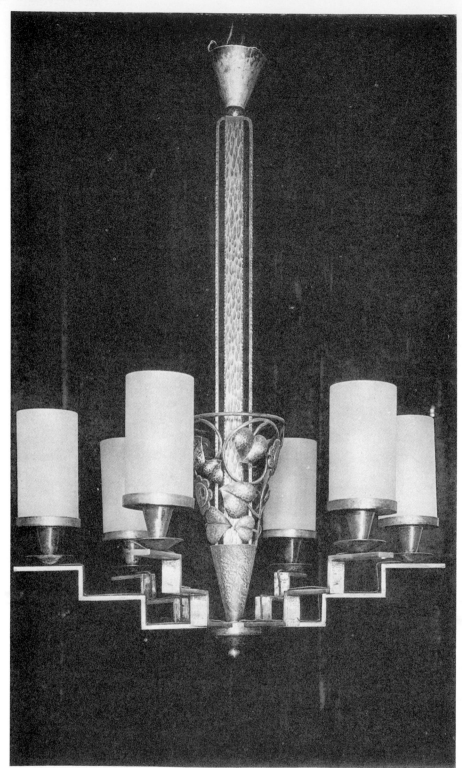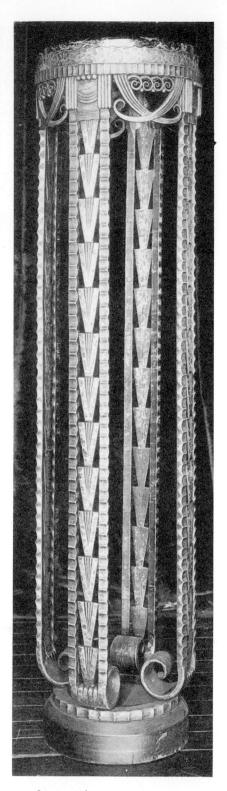

54. (Left) Chandelier. (Right) Floor lamp. Bergue, designer of ironwork.

55. Interior grillwork. Paul Kiss, ironwork designer.

56. Wrought iron staircase in a large store. Raymond Subes, ironwork designer. Patout, architect.

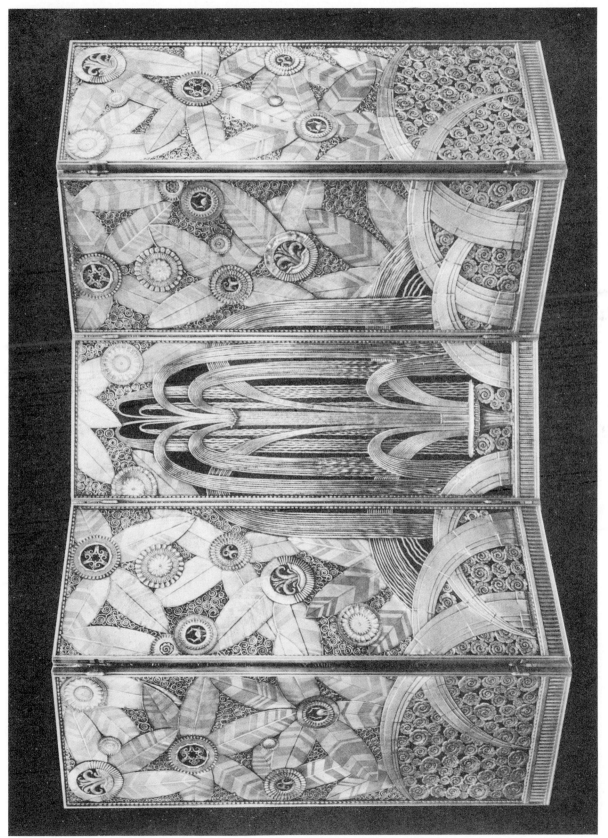

57. Folding screen, "The Oasis," (Wrought iron highlighted with gold). Edgar Brandt, ironwork designer.

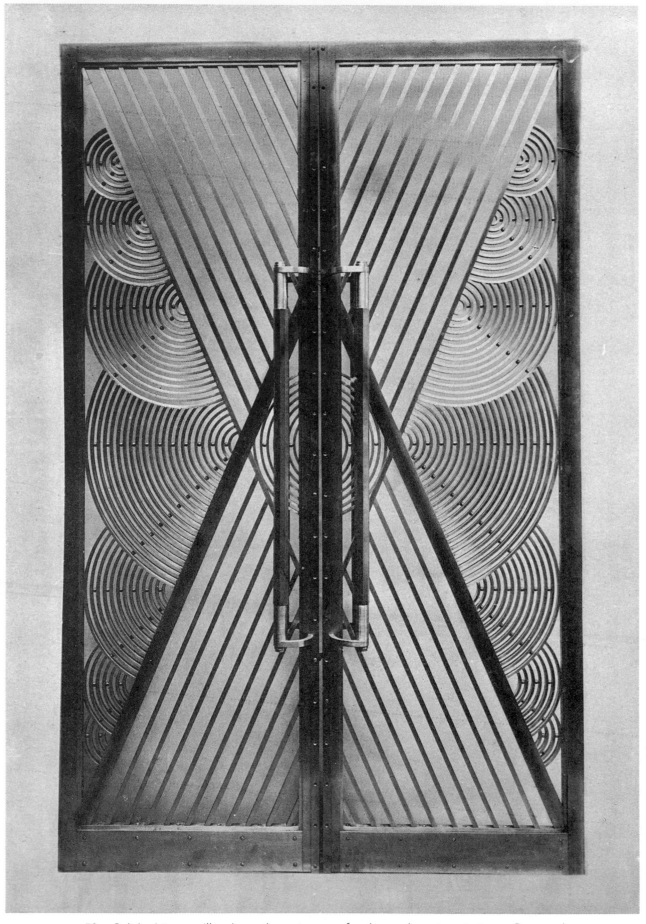

58. Polished iron grillwork on the entrance of a large department store. Raymond Subes, ironwork designer. Patout, architect.

59.   (Top) Interior grillwork. Lamp stands. Edgar Brandt, ironwork designer. (Bottom)
Interior grillwork. Edgar Brandt, ironwork designer.

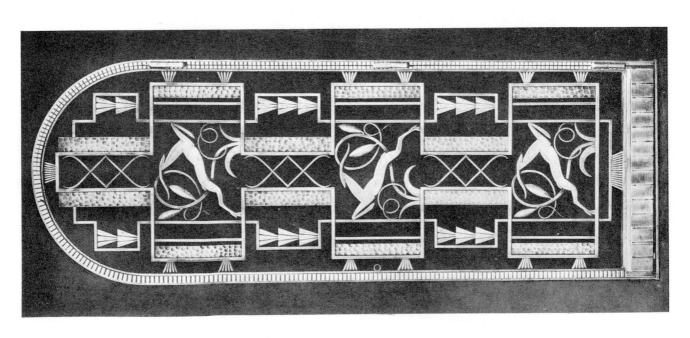

60. Interior doors. Edgar Brandt, ironwork designer.

61. (Top) Building entrance. J. Bertrand, architect. Raymond Subes, ironwork designer. (Bottom) Mirror and table. Raymond Subes, designer.

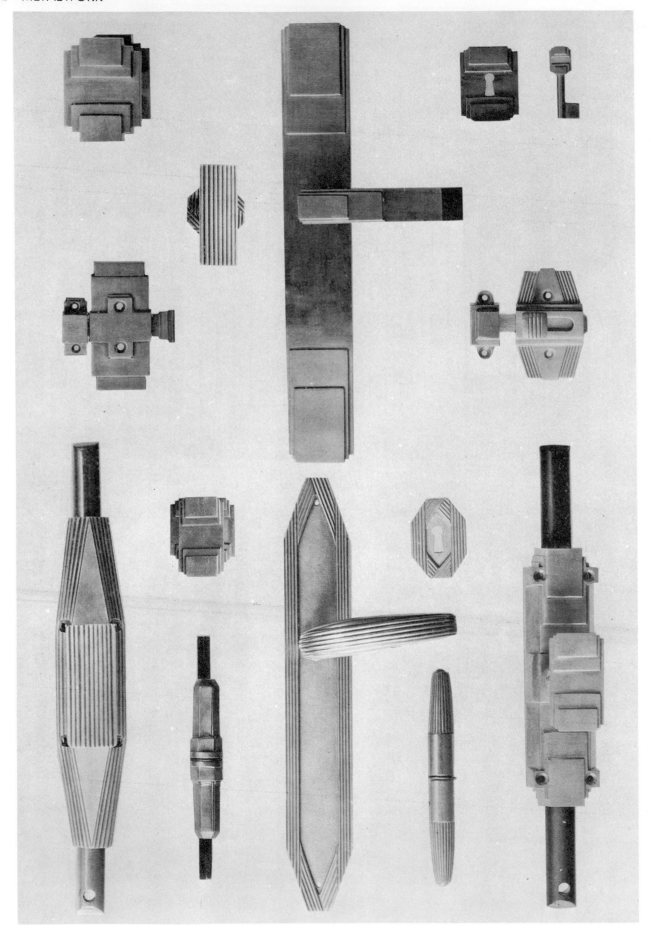

62. Latches and locks. Jean Puiforcat and Dominique, designers.

63.   Main staircase in the City Hall, Rheims. Bouchette and Expert, architects. Raymond Subes, ironwork designer.

64. Dining room of the "Pavillon de la Maîtrise," Paris Exhibition, 1925. Maurice Dufrène, designer. Ironwork by Vasseur.

65. Sanatorium, Hilversum, Netherlands. Byvoet and Duiker, architects.

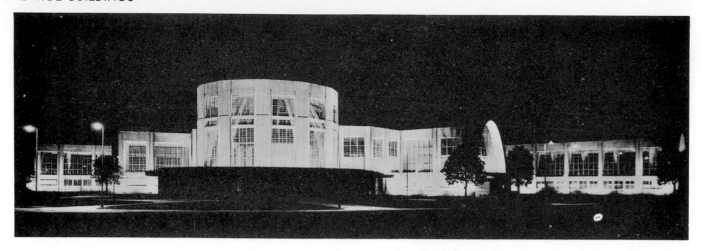

66.   Exhibition of Contemporary Culture, Brno. (Top) Central Hall. Jar Valenta,
Engineer. (Middle) Entrance. Emil Karilik, architect. (Bottom) Moravian Pavilion.
Joseph Fuchs, architect.

67. Pavilion of the City of Brno. Joseph Fuchs, architect.

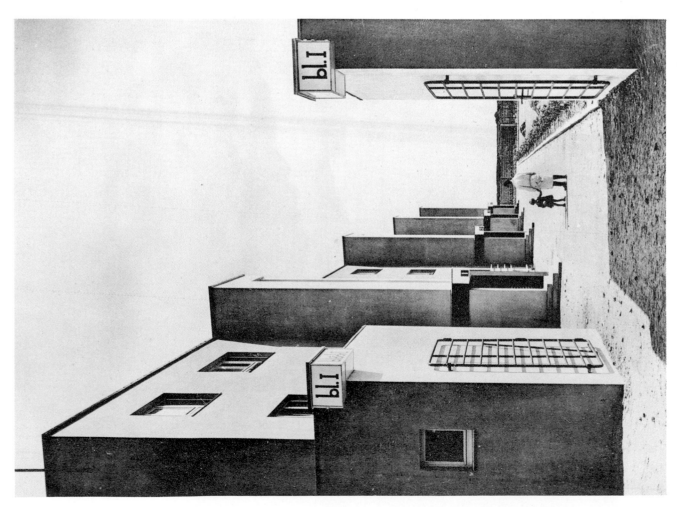

68. Row of houses, Celle, Germany. Otto Haesler, architect.

69. Central Market, Rheims. Emile Maigrot, architect.

70. Design for an apartment complex to be built on the banks of the Seine. Henri Sauvage, architect.

71. Workers' homes, Hermsdorf, Germany. Thilo Schoder, architect.

72. (Top left) Exposition hall. Bruno Taut, architect. (Top right) Indoor tennis court, Copenhagen. Christiani and Nielsen, architects. (Bottom left) Market, Frankfurt/a./Main. Martin Elsaesser, architect. (Bottom right) Workshop at Chemnitz train station. Kell and Löser, architects.

73. Schools, Hilversum, Netherlands. W. M. Dudok, architect.

74.   Design for the Hilversum city hall. W. M. Dudok, architect.

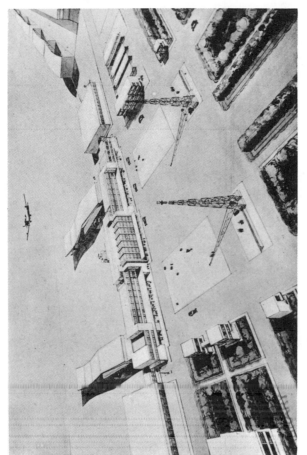

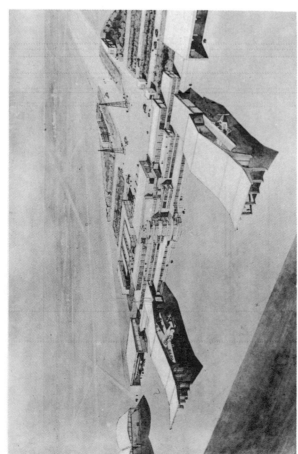

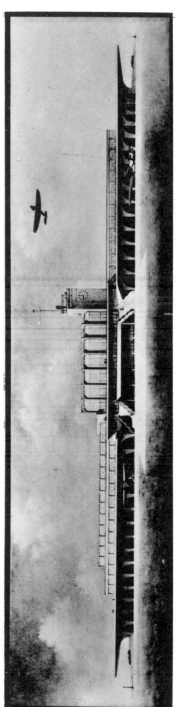

75. Airport Plans. (Top and bottom) J. Ginsberg. (Middle) Louis Iturralde.

76. (Left) New York Telephone Company Building, New York. Kenzie, Voorhees and Gmelin, architects. (Right) General Motors Building, New York. Shreve and Lamb, architects.

77.   Interior of the Esders factory. A. and G. Perret, architects.

78. Capitol Movie Theater, Berlin. Hans Poelzig, architect.

79.   Movie auditorium in the Aubette, Strasbourg.   Théo Van Doesburg, architect.

80. Two views of the "Voisin Plan" for a contemporary city. Le Corbusier and P. Jeanneret, architects.

81.   Rug.   Sonia Delaunay.

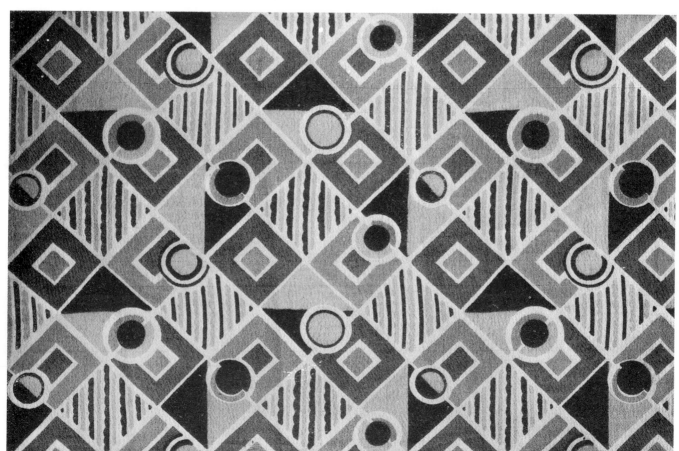

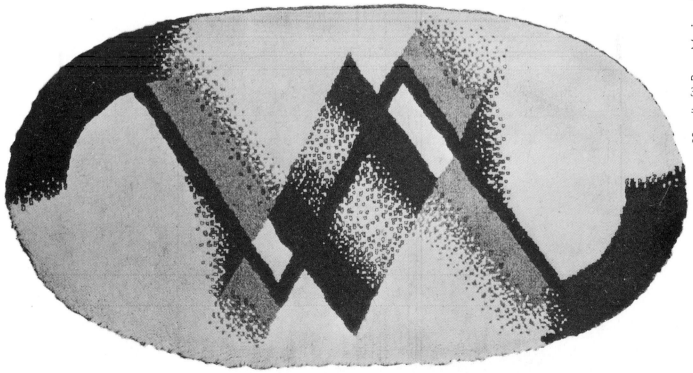

83. (Left) Rug. Mariane Clouzot. (Right) Rug. Marguerite Dubuisson.

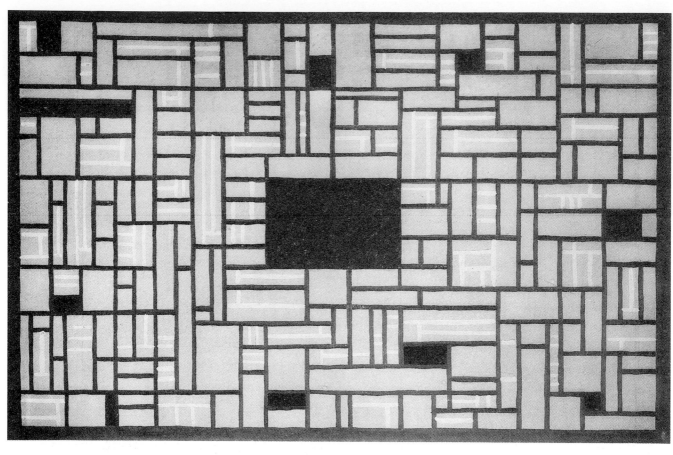

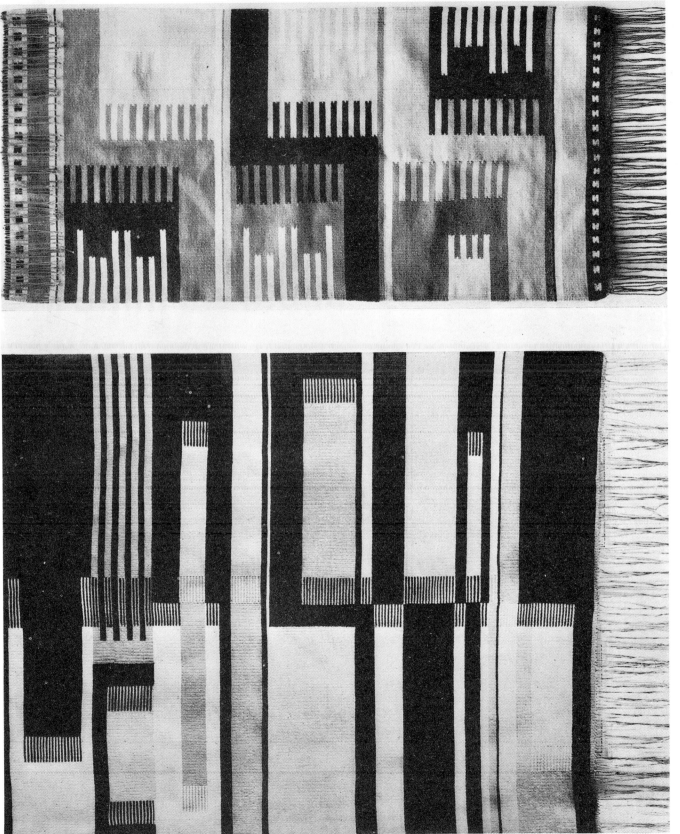

85. Rugs. Richard Herre.

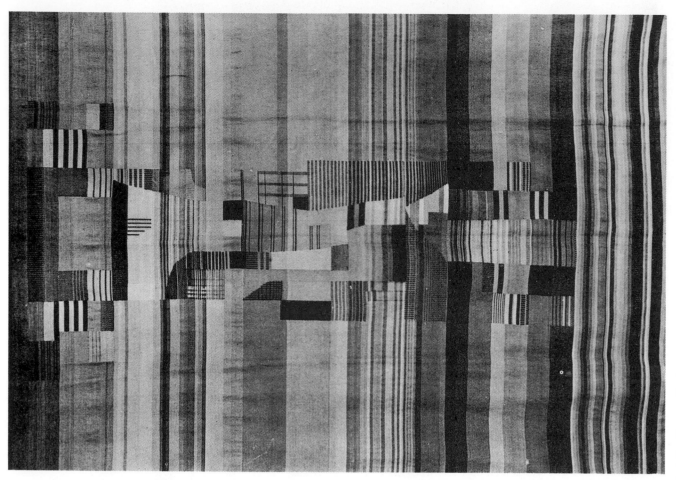

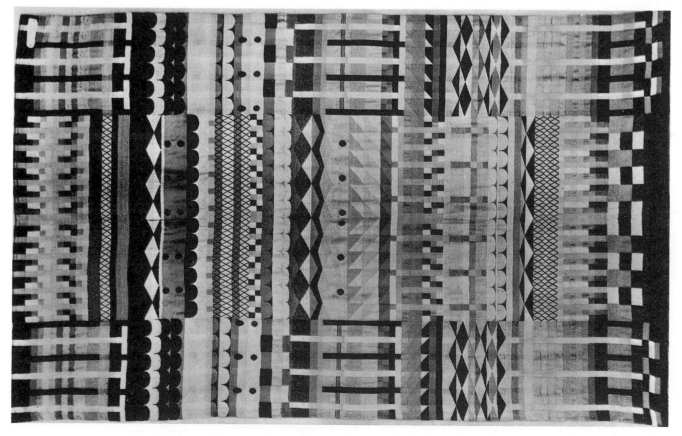

86. Rugs. Strobel at the Dessau Bauhaus.

87. Rug. Da Silva Bruhns.

88. (Left) Fabric. Maurice Dufrène. (Right) Fabric. Pierre Legrain.

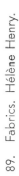

89. Fabrics. Hélène Henry.

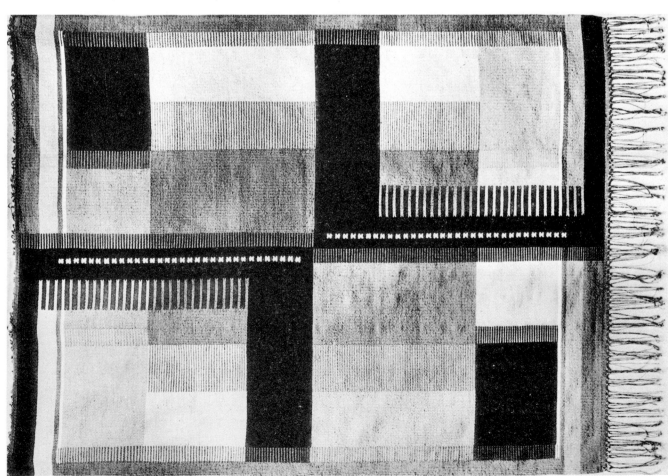

90. (Left) Rug. Richard Herre. (Right) Rug. Martha Erps at the Weimar Bauhaus.

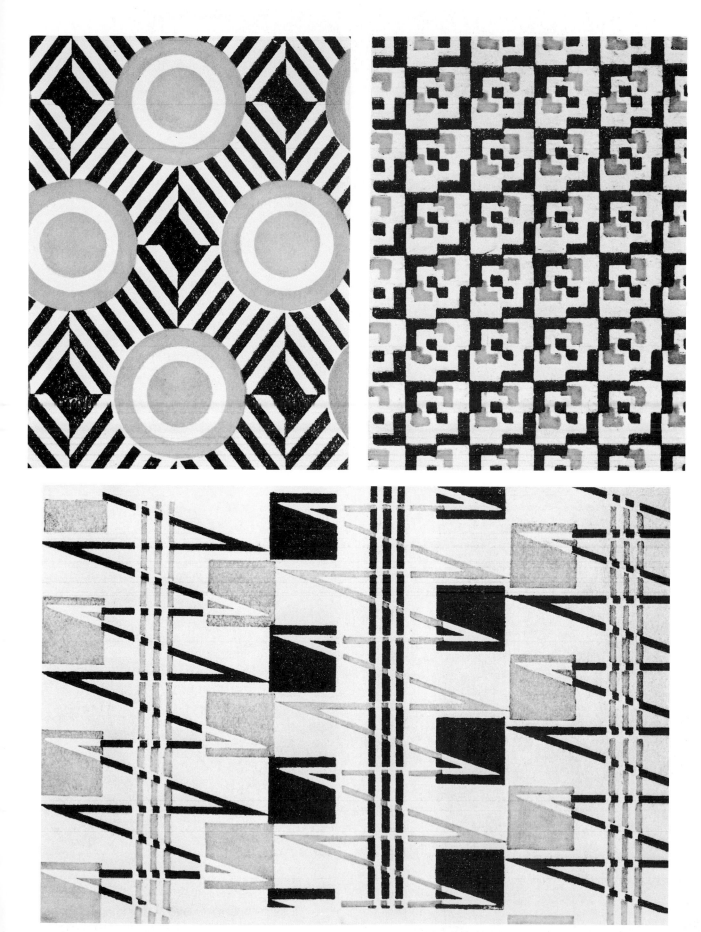

91. Russian wallpaper. (Left and lower right) Stepanova. (Upper right) Popova.

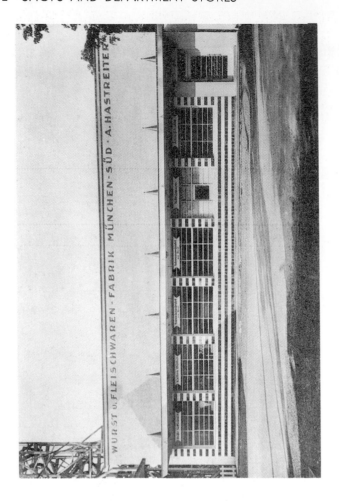

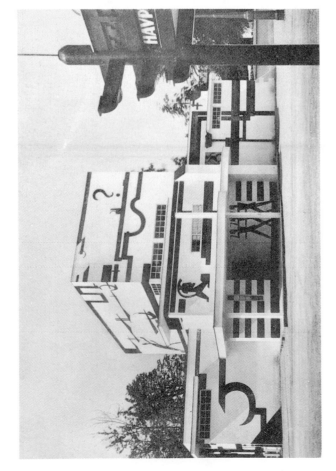

92. Pavilions at the Munich Exposition. Max Wiederanders, architect.

93. Interior of the Israel Department Store, Berlin. Heinrich Straumer, architect.

94.   Facade of the Bally Shoe Store, Paris.   Robert Mallet-Stevens, architect.

95.   Facade of the Isabey Perfume Shop, Paris. Ch. Siclis, architect.

96.   Pierre Legrain, designer.

97.   Georges Crette, designer.

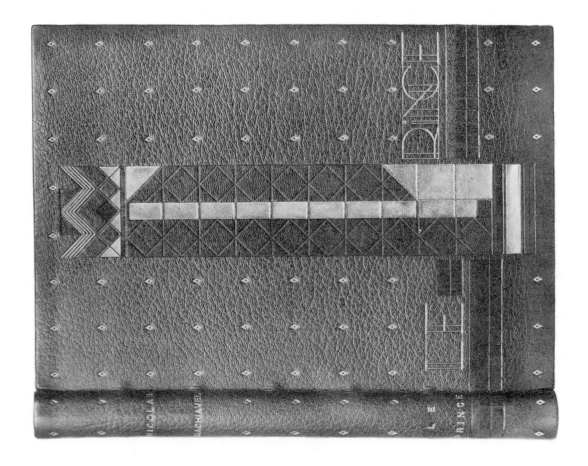

98. Pierre Legrain, designer.

99. Paul Bonet, designer.

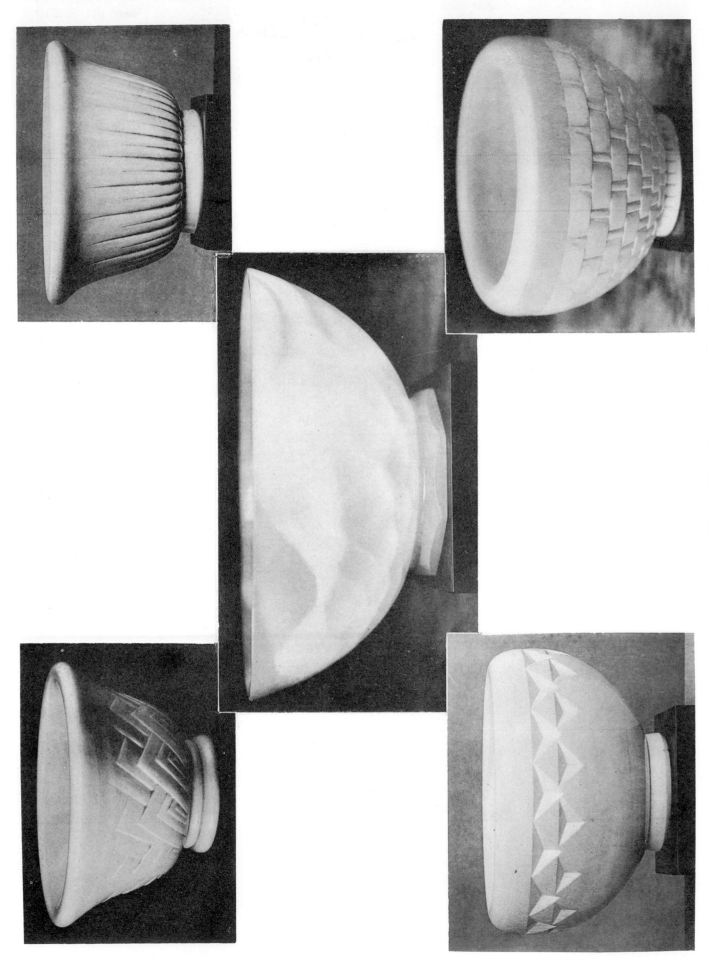

100.   Four carved ivory bowls. (Center) Bowl of mauve agate. George Bastard.

101. Chess set in silver, ivory and ebony. Jean Puiforcat.

102.   Large pieces of deeply cut glass.   Maurice Marinot.

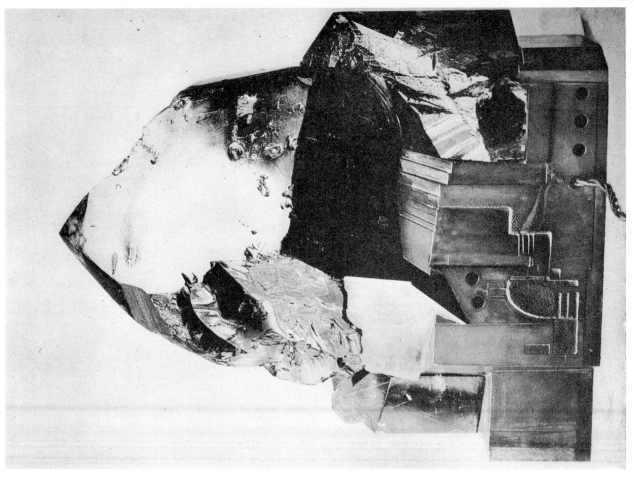

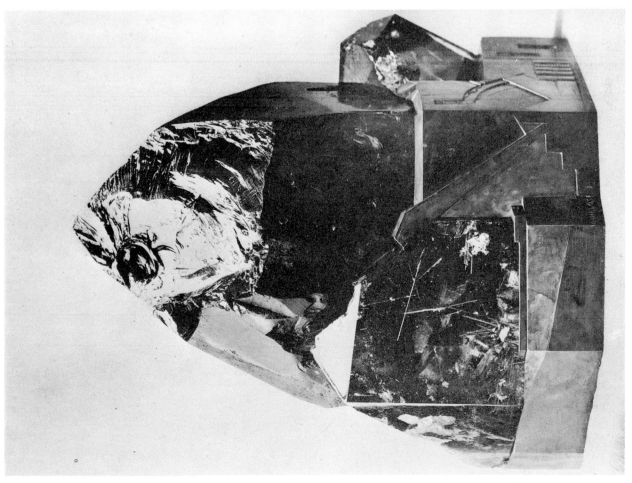

103.   Smoked rock crystal lit on the inside in green. Gustave Miklos.

104.   Metalwork. Claudius Linossier, for Rouard.

105.   (Top) Silvered bronze bird on a marble base. Josef Csaky. (Bottom) Amethyst mounted on Belgian granite; the whole forming a flower. Josef Csaky.

106.   Mother-of-pearl fans. George Bastard.

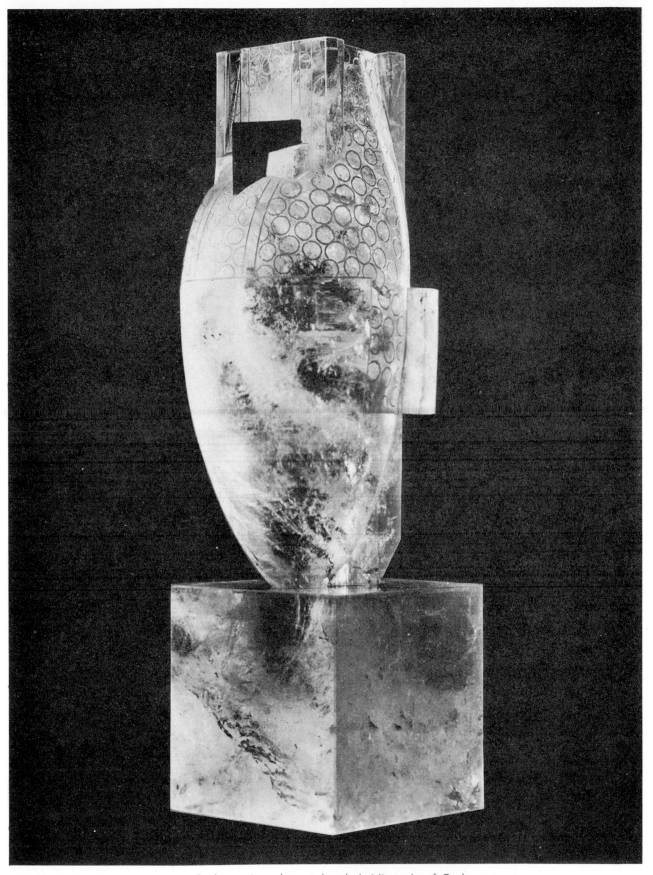

107.   Sculpture in rock crystal and obsidian. Josef Csaky.

108.   Posters.   Edward MacKnight Kauffer.

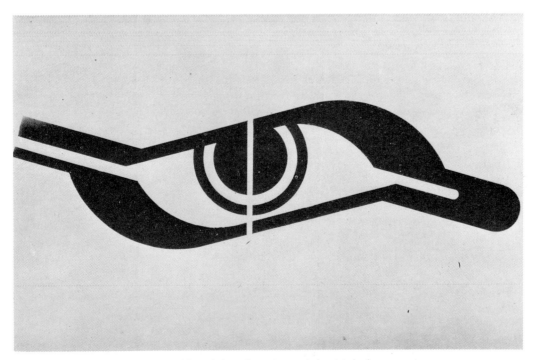

109. Advertisements. Johs. Molzahn.

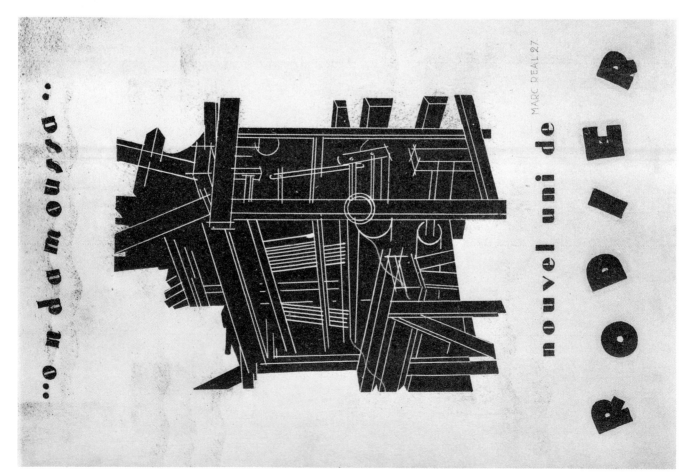

110. Advertisements. Marc Réal.

III. Poster. Jan Mucharski.

112. Poster. Otto Morach.

113. Poster. Jean Carlu.

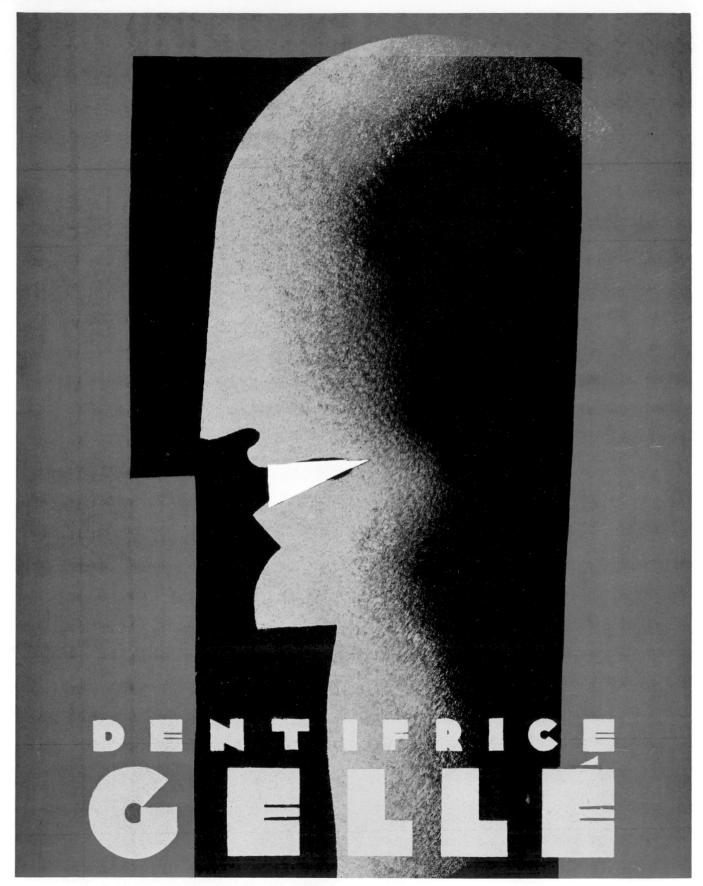

114. Poster. Jean Carlu.

115.   Poster.   Austin Cooper.

116.   Dust wrapper.   Herbert Bayer.

117. Poster. A. M. Cassandre.

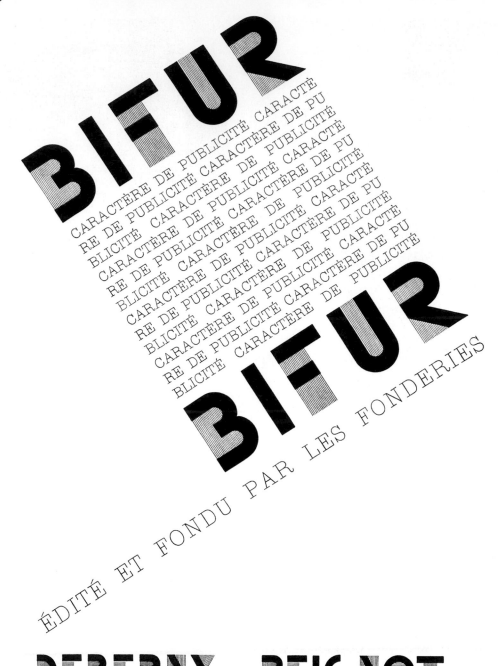

118. Type specimen. A. M. Cassandre.

119. Catalog covers. Libis

120. Poster. A. Mahlau.

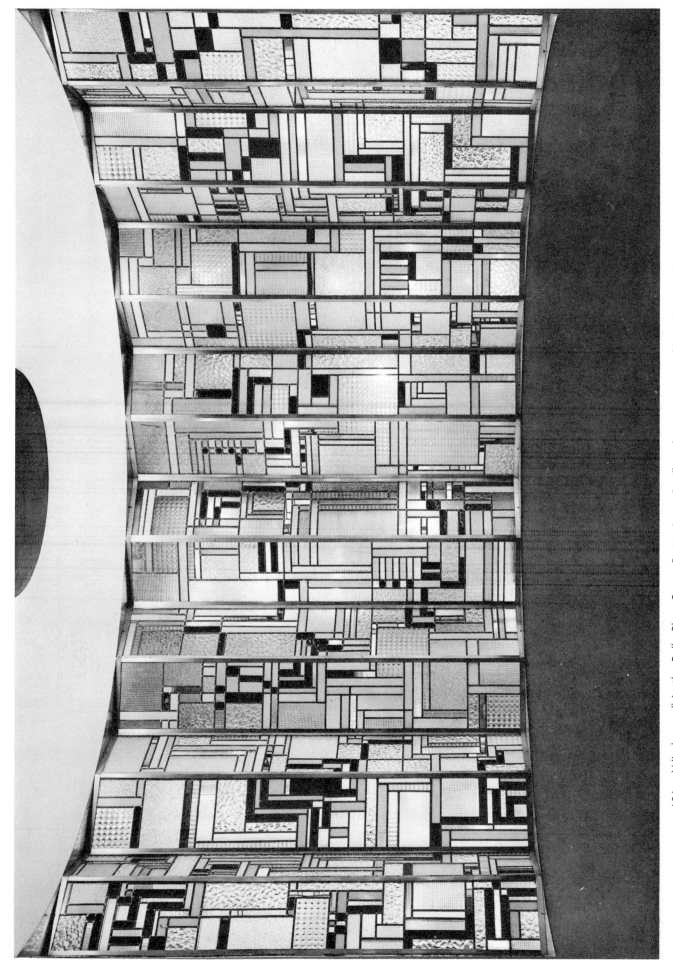

121. Window wall in the Bally Shoe Store, Paris. Louis Barillet, designer. J. Le Chevalier and Th. Hanssen, associates. Robert Mallet-Stevens, architect.

122. Details of stained glass windows, Frankfurt/a./Main. Executed by the Puhl and Wagner Company after a design by Peter Roehl.

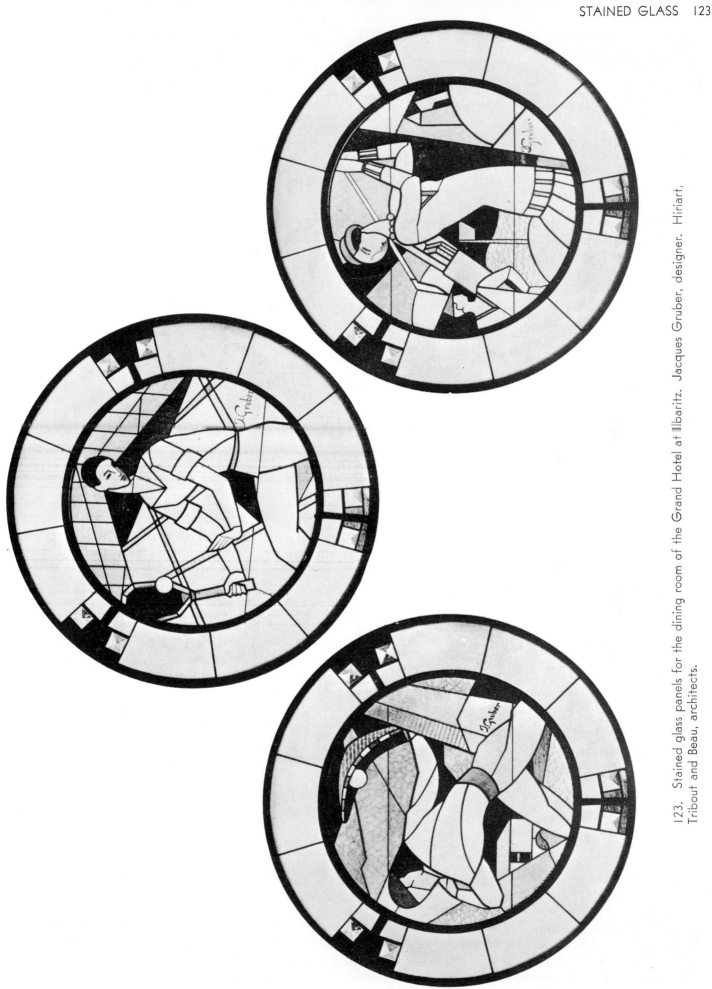

123.   Stained glass panels for the dining room of the Grand Hotel at Ilbaritz. Jacques Gruber, designer. Hiriart, Tribout and Beau, architects.

124. Window wall in the stairwell of the Radio Bar. Designed by Maurice Jallot.
Executed by Hagnauer and Maurice Jallot.

125. Two stained glass works by J. Gaudin. (Left) "Seascape" after a sketch by L. Mazetier. (Right) "Twilight" after a sketch by Elesz Kiervicz.

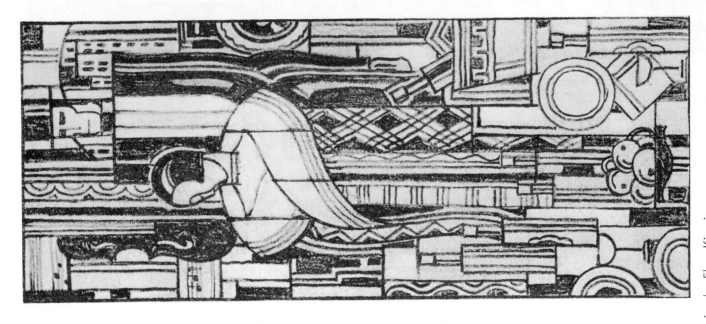

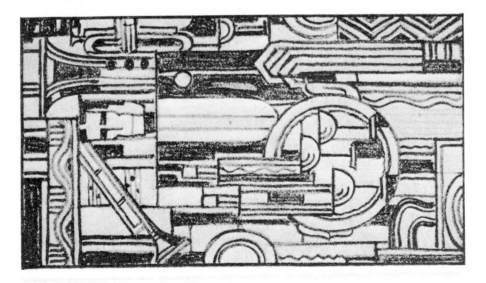

126. Stained glass windows for a restaurant. J. Gaudin after a design by Elesz Kiervicz.

127. Stained glass window for a publishing house. Jacques Gruber.

128. Stained glass windows. Jaap Gidding.

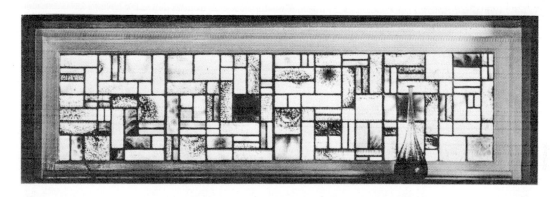

129. Stained glass windows. Executed after designs by A. D. Copier. Manufactured at the Leerdam Glassworks, Netherlands.

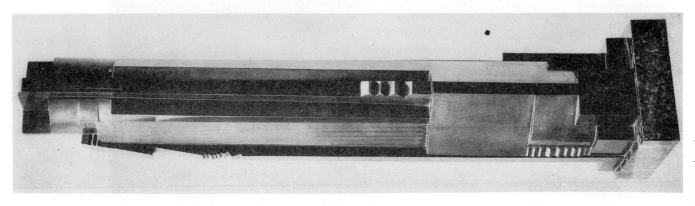

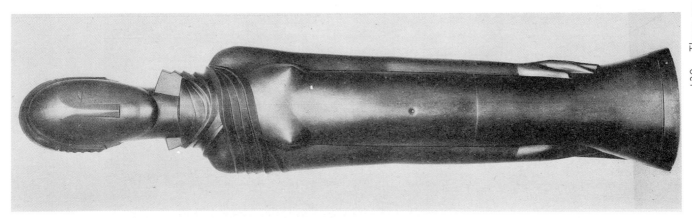

130. Three sculptures by Gustave Miklos. (Left) Bronze. (Middle) Woman with bird (bas-relief in pink cement set with enamelled disks and framed in iron). (Right) Architectural bronze sculpture in honor of Franz Liszt.

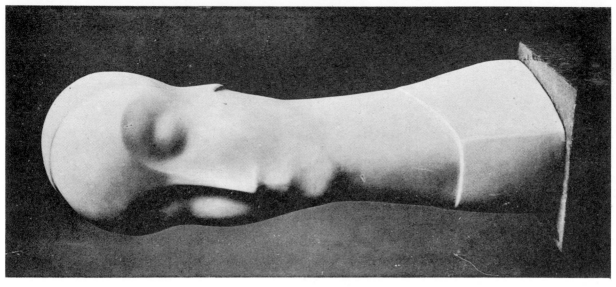

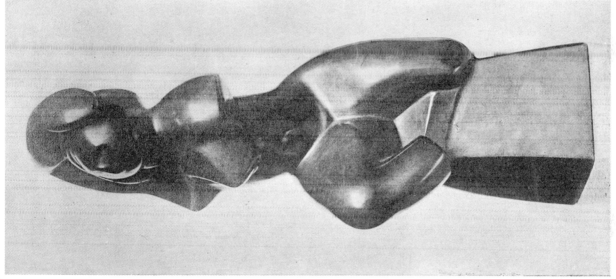

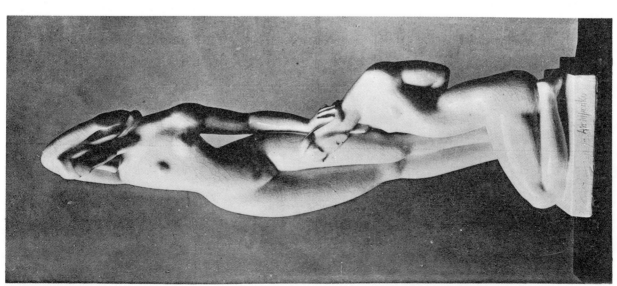

131. Three sculptures by Alexandre Archipenko. (Left) Group (ceramic). (Middle) Bronze. (Right) Head (marble).

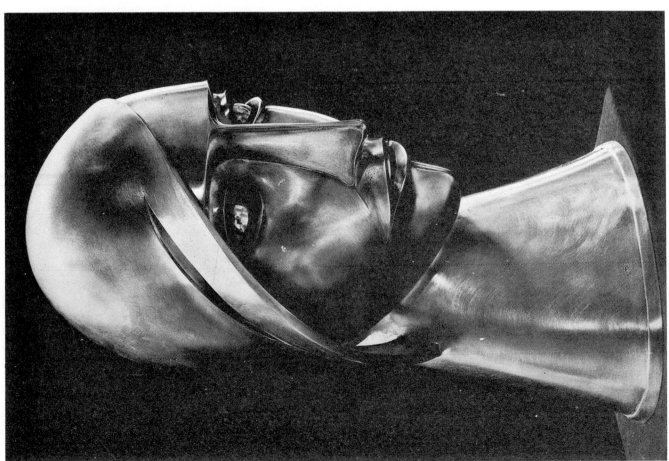

132. (Left) Head (copper). Rudolf Belling. (Right) Head in repoussé copper. Hans Wissel.

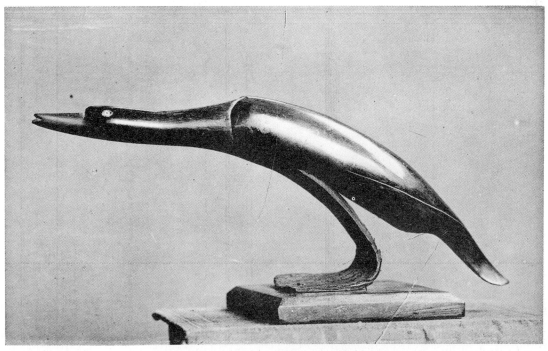

133. Birds of carved horn from Madagascar.

134. Two sculptures by Irène Codréano. (Left) Chinese girl in marble. (Right) Portrait in marble.

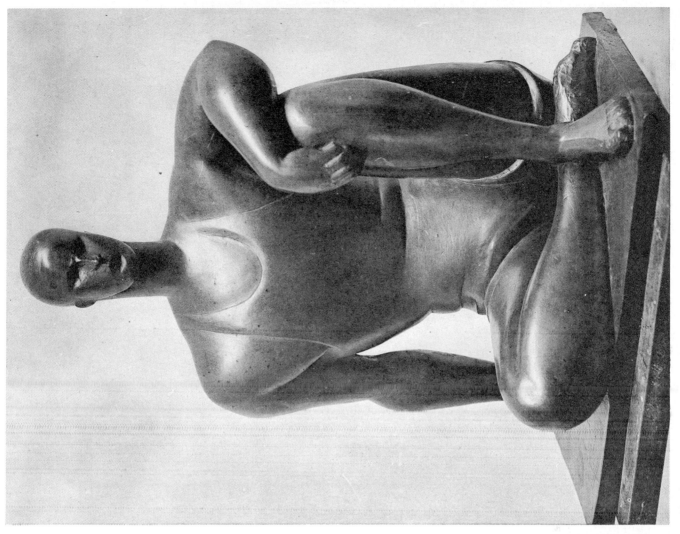

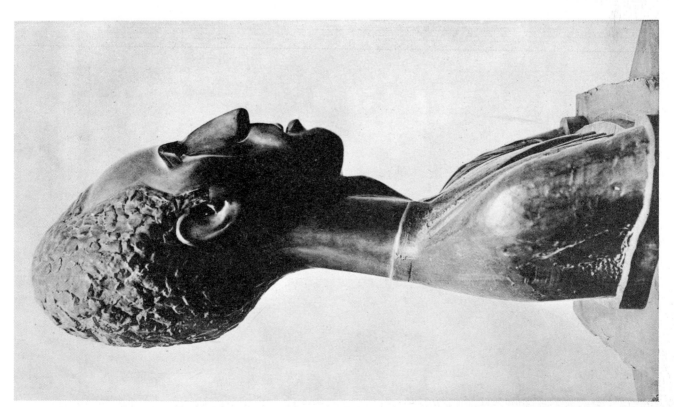

135. Two sculptures by Chana Orloff. (Left) Portrait in bronze. (Right) Bather in bronze.

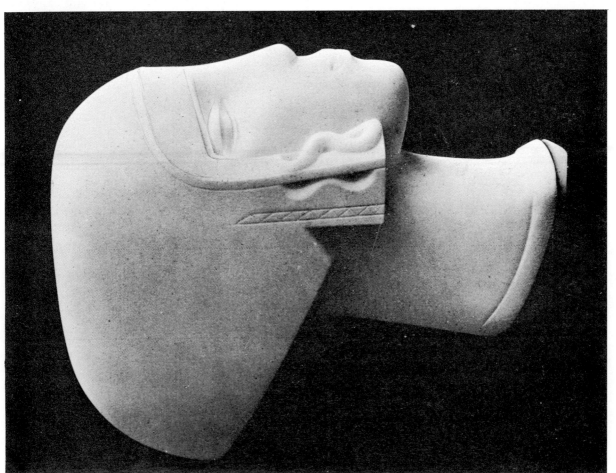

136. (Left) Marble head. Josef Csaky. (Right) Mannequin. André Vigneau.

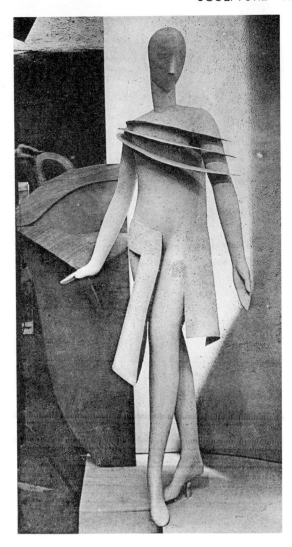

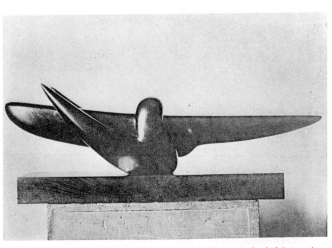

137.   (Top left) Mother and child in ebony. Chauvin. (Top right) Mannequin. André Vigneau. (Bottom left) Ebony sculpture. Chauvin. (Bottom right) Sculpture. Otto Gutfreund.

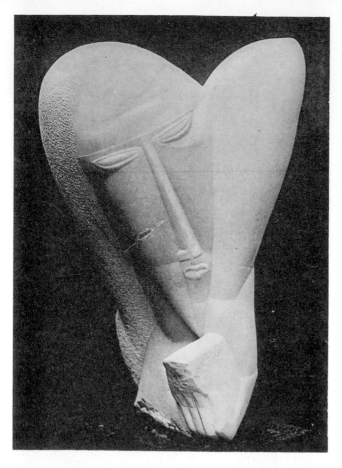

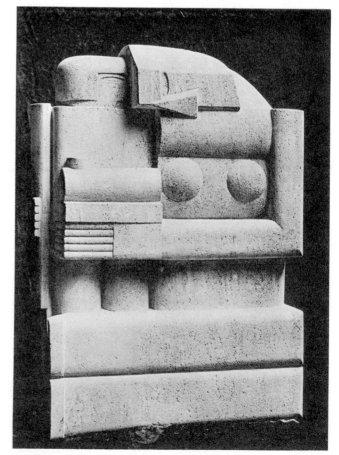

138.   Four sculptures by Oscar Jespers. (Top left) Object in marble. (Top right) Girl in marble. (Bottom left) Seated nude in stone. (Bottom right) Toy in stone.

139. Three sculptures by Gustave Miklos. (Left) Bronze sculpture. (Middle) Clown (polychrome bronze). (Right) Bronze sculpture.

. Desny.

141.   Grey faïence dishes decorated with shiny platinum.   Jean Luce.

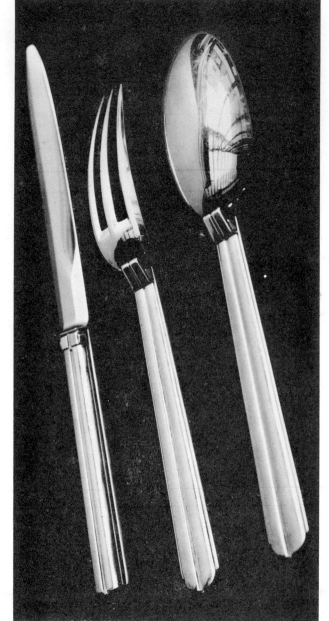

142.   Flatware. Jean Puiforcat.

143.   Cocktail set.   Desny.

144. Cut crystal and ebony bottles. Gaston L. Vuitton.

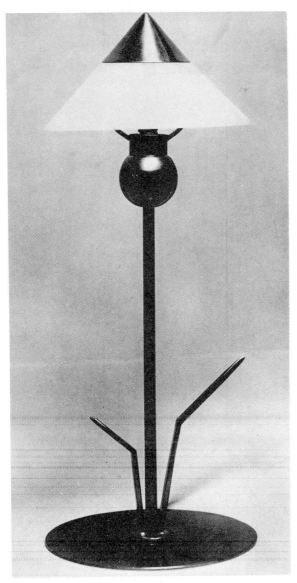

145.   (Upper left and bottom) Lamps. Marc Erol. (Upper right) Lamps. I. Ch. Goetz.

146. Pillows. Madame Jean Tranchant.

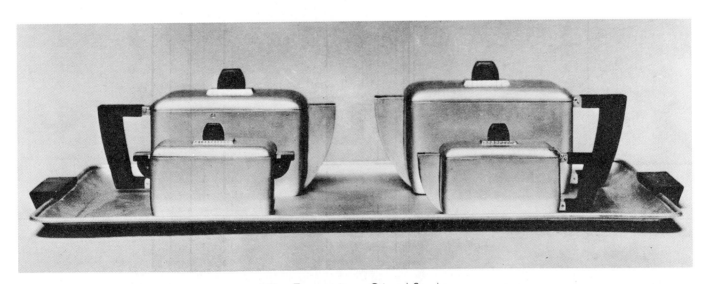

147. Tea services. Gérard Sandoz.

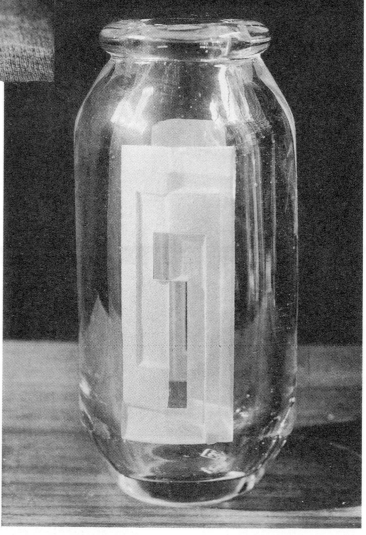

148. Cut glass vases. Jean Luce.

149. Lighting fixtures. Desny.

150. Lighting fixture. Desny.

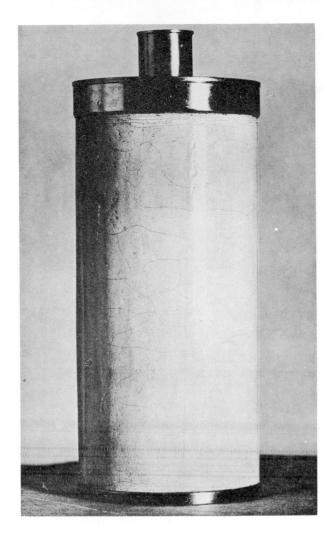

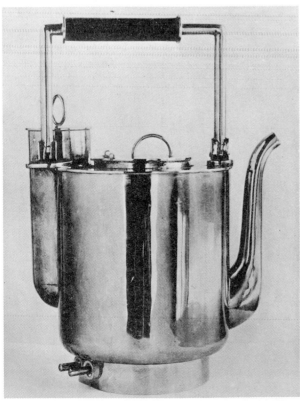

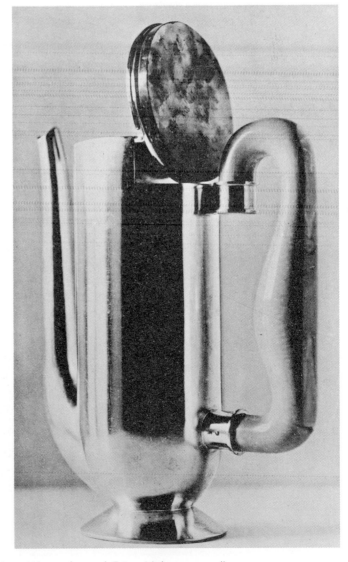

151. (Upper left) White tea canister. Hans Warnecke and Erica Habermann. (Lower left) Electric teapot in silver. Wolfgang Tümpel. (Upper right and lower right) Teapot and coffeepot. Gold base, ivory handles, chrysoprase lids. Wolfgang Tümpel.

152. Mirrors. Desny.

153. (Top) Cut crystal and ebony bottle. Suzanne Auzanneau and Gaston L. Vuitton.
(Bottom) Brush case in silver and ebony. Suzanne Auzanneau and Gaston L. Vuitton.

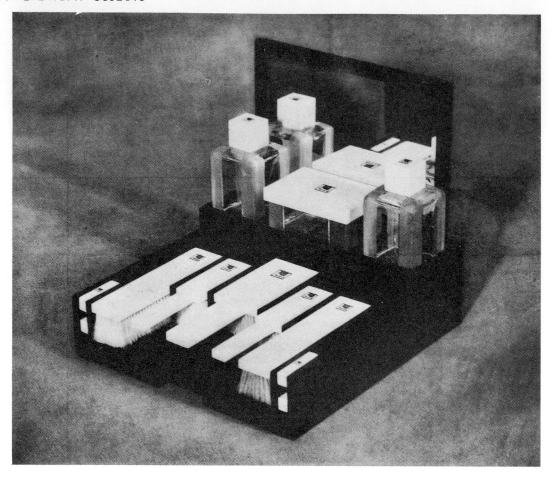

154.   Cases for brushes and bottles.   Gaston L. Vuitton.

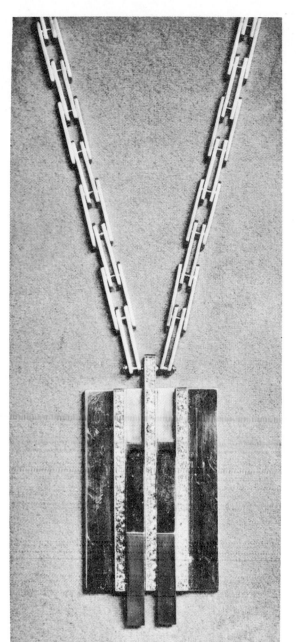

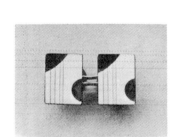

155.   Cuff links, brooches, pendant and bracelet. Jean Fouquet.

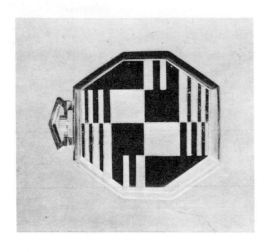

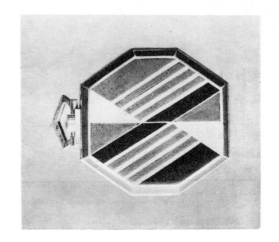

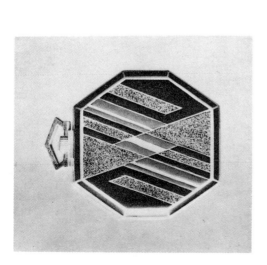

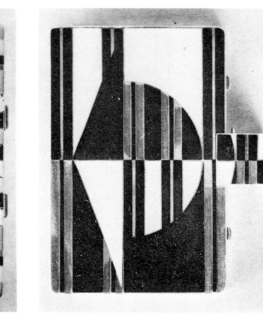

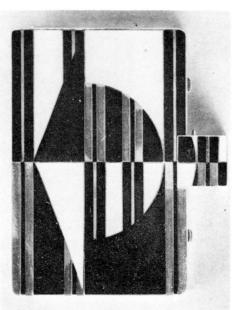

156. Pocket watches and cases. Gérard Sandoz.

157. Bracelets, brooch and ring. Gérard Sandoz.

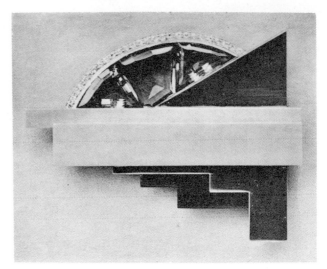

158. Brooches and bracelets. Jean Fouquet.

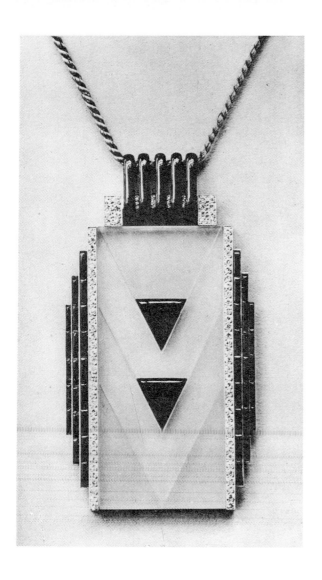

159. (Top) Pendants. Eric Gragge. (Bottom) Vanity case. Jean Fouquet.

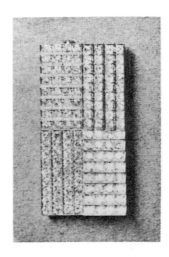

160.   Rings, pendant, brooches and bracelet. Jean Fouquet.

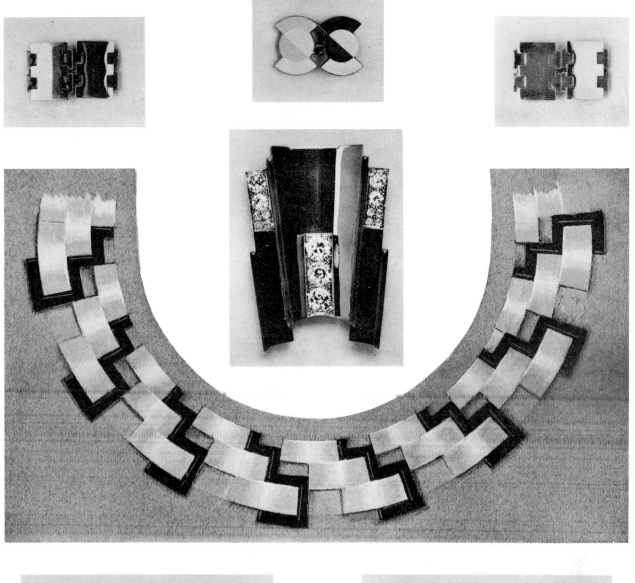

161. Cuff links, brooches, bracelets and design for a necklace. Raymond Templier.

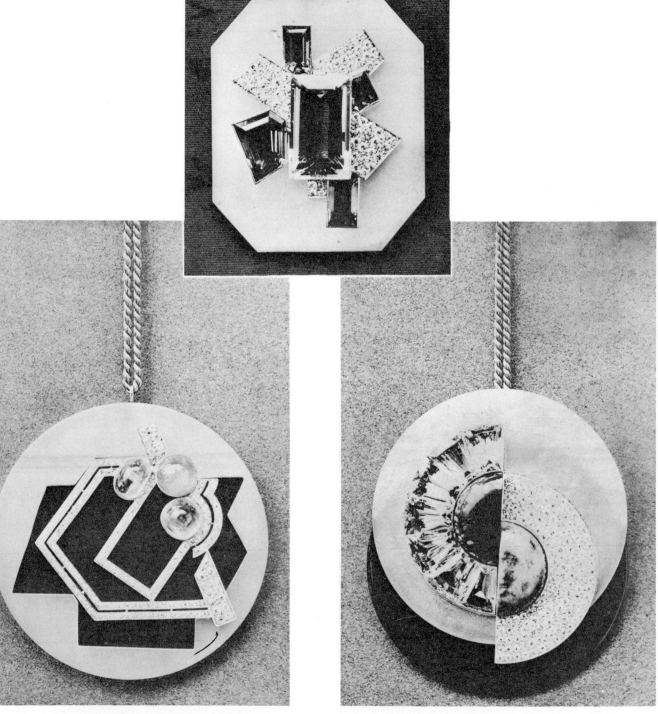

162. (Top and bottom left) Pendants. A. Léveillé. (Bottom right) Pendant. Designed by E. Mouron. Executed by Georges Fouquet.

163.   Boxes, vanity cases and cigarette cases.   Paul Brandt.

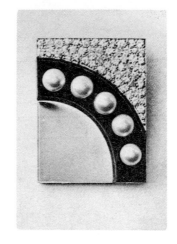

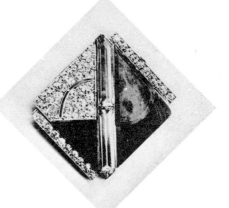

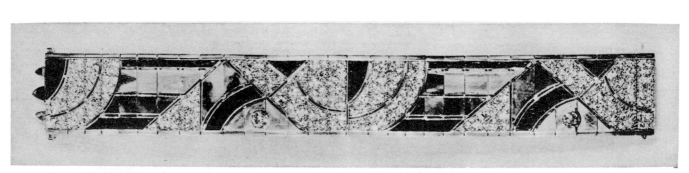

164. Hat ornaments, brooches and bracelet. Paul Brandt.

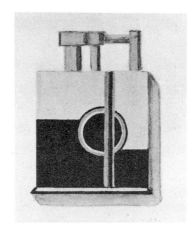

165. Designs for brooches, cigarette case, cigarette lighter and bracelet. Yolande Mas.

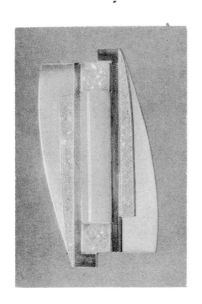
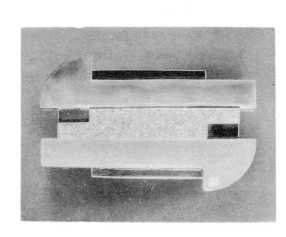
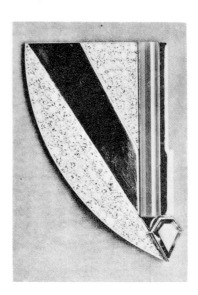

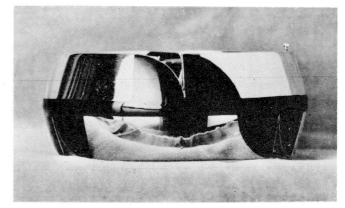

166.   Earrings, rings, brooches and bracelets. Raymond Templier.

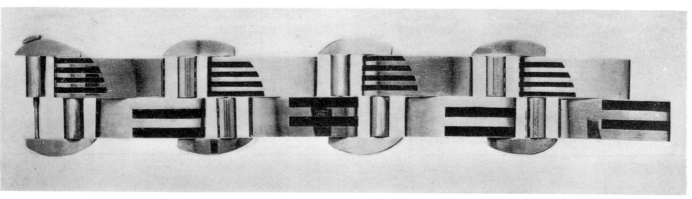

167. Bracelets. Gérard Sandoz.

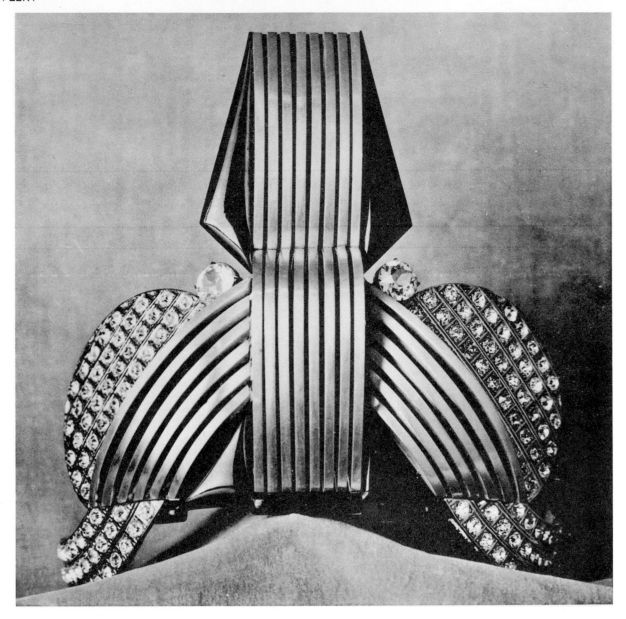

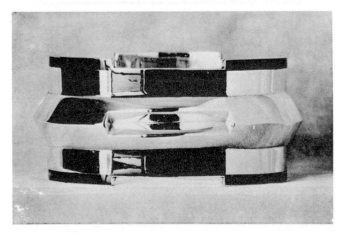 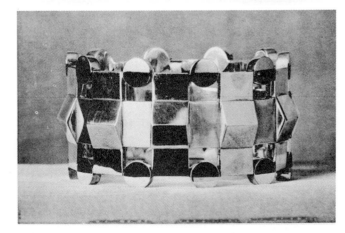

168. Crown designed for Brigitte Helm in the film "L'Argent." Bracelets. Raymond Templier.

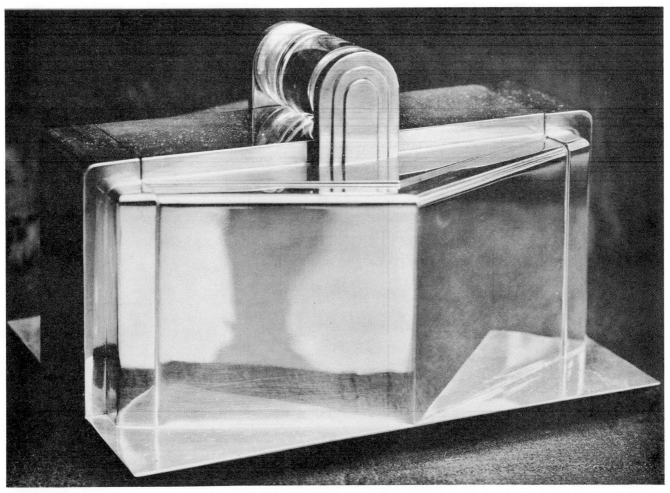

169. (Top) Silver Box. (Bottom) Cookie box.

170. (1) Detail of the façade of the French Pavilion at the Milan Fair. (L. Boileau, architect) Sculpture by Binquet. (2) Door panel with wood carving. Sculpture by Binquet. (3 & 4) Models of two medallions to be executed in stone for the facade of the Post Office at Casablanca. (Laforge, architect) Sculpture by Binquet.

171. Bas-reliefs in the dining room at the Embassy Pavilion, Paris Exhibition, 1925.
(H. Rapin, architect). (Top) Presentation of the credentials. Sculpture by Max-Blondat.
(Bottom) Arrival of the ambassador. Sculpture by Max-Blondat.

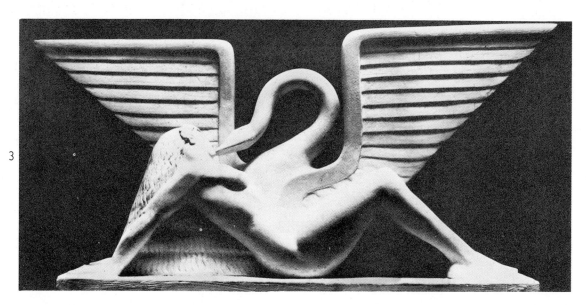

172. (1) Motif adorning the vestibule of honor at the Pavilion of the City of Paris. Sculpture by Bouraine. (2) Decorative masque on the facade of the Pavilion of the City of Paris. Sculpture by Bouraine. (3) A Leda in silvered and oxidized bronze. Sculpture by Bouraine. (4) Turbots swimming through sea weed. Sculpture by Bouraine.

173. (1,2) Mirror pediments. (3,5) Door panels. (4) Capital for the facade of the Elysèe-Palace Hotel. (6) Overdoor. Sculptures by Camille Garnier.

174. (1) Shelf clock. Albert Guénot. (2, 3, 4) Panels. Albert Guénot. '(5) Panelled
sideboard. Albert Guénot, in collaboration with Paul Follot.

1

2   3

175. (1) "Harmony: Homage to Jean Goujon." Sculpture by Janniot. (2, 3) High relief (haut relief) "Eros" details. Sculpture by Janniot.

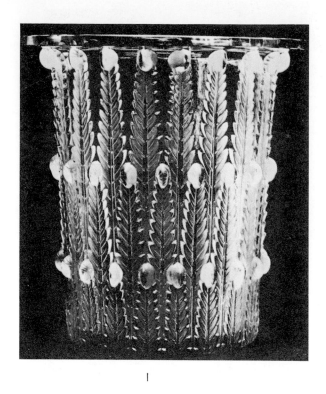

1

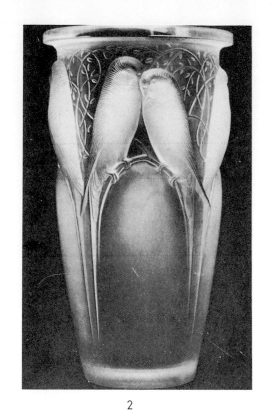

2

3

4

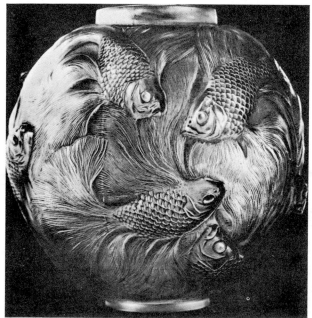

176. Vases in molded glass. René Lalique. (1) medlar-tree (2) parakeets (3) fish
(4) mistletoe.

177. Sculptures by Joël and Jan Martel. (1) King Arthur. (2) The Island of Avalon (stone carving). (3) Statue for the monument to Claude Debussy. (4, 6) Bas-reliefs from the smoking room of the Embassy Pavilion, Paris Exhibition, 1925. (5) The dancer, Malkowsky. (7) Sculpture for the bathroom at the Sèvres Porcelain Manufactory.

1

2

3

4

5

178. (1, 5) Bas-reliefs from the Tourism Pavilion. (Robert Mallet-Stevens, architect).
Joël and Jan Martel. (2, 3, 4) Bas-reliefs on the Concorde door. Joël and Jan Martel.

1

2

3

4

5

6

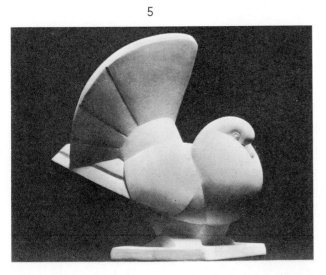

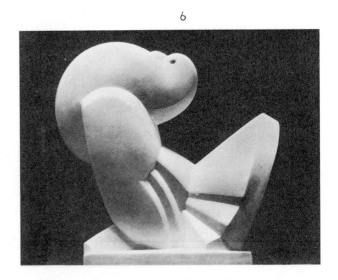

179.   Sculptures by Joël and Jan Martel. (1) weasel (2) cat (3) magpie (4) bird (5 & 6) pigeons.

180. Chapel in the Polish section. Designed by Jean Szczepowski. Executed by the Second Municipal Crafts School in Varsovie under the direction of Francis Tokarski.

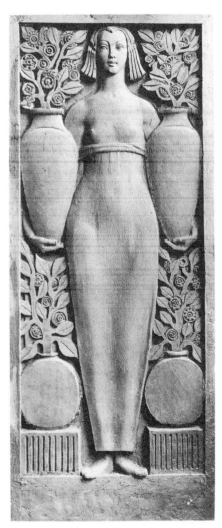

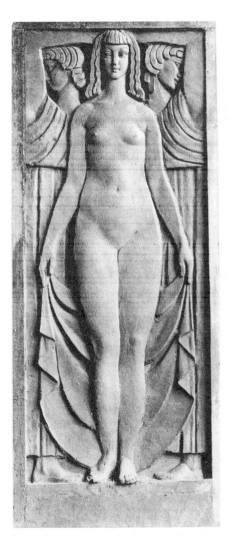

181. (1, 2) Bas-reliefs for a tavern. (Gaillard, architect) Sculpture by Bouraine. (3, 4) Bas-reliefs for the Pavilion of the City of Paris. (Bouvard, architect) Sculpture by Bouraine and Le Faguays.

182. Sculptures by Gauvenet. (1) Engraved porcelain lamp shade. (2, 4) Engraved porcelain vases. (3) Lamp with engraved porcelain shade and metal stand. (5, 6, 7) Porcelain statues designed to be painted. (8) Porcelain frieze. (9, 10, 11) Porcelain plaques for an illuminated ceiling. All of the figures reproduced on this page are from the Sèvres Porcelain Manufactory.

INDEX
OF ARTISTS